Doubleday Science Fiction, 1969 / title font: Huxley Vertical

"I think the 60s and 70s were probably one the most creatively interesting periods for everyone. Art, music, film all pushing the envelope. New York City was affordable and fun, fertile in its influences. Book cover art, book jacket art was fun concept art, a bit more free than other illustration work." (From a 2016 interview by Joachim Boaz. See sciencefictionruminations.com)

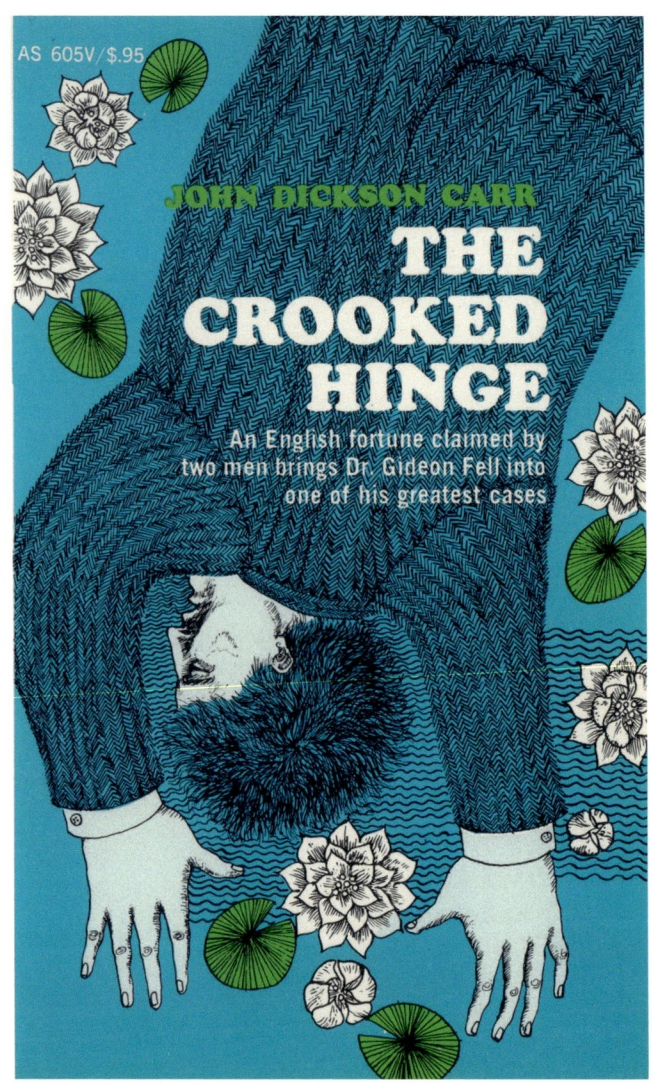

Collier Books, c1966 / title font: Cooper Black

"*The Corpse in the Waxworks* and *The Crooked Hinge* were my first two book covers . . . [I] hardly knew what I was doing and had to have help with the fonts."

Collier Books, c1960s / title font: Bookman

"I started doing book covers early on for a Pratt friend who was an art director for Collier Books mystery paperbacks. I really knew nothing about the process. The artist was responsible for illustration, design, typography, and color separation . . . Another Pratt friend helped with the type and taught me how to do a paste up and mechanical." (interview by Joachim Boaz)

Doubleday Science Fiction, 1967 / title font: Venus Bold

"My favorite cover I think is for *The Night Spiders*. A close second is *Froomb*. Coincidentally both books are by John Lymington. *Froomb* is I believe my first for Doubleday, but my memory is a bit fuzzy."

Doubleday Science Fiction, 1966 / title font: Haas Inserat-Grotesk

"I think the fact that the covers were printed in black and two colors readily adapted to something more graphic. Composition and color combination could add to an atmospheric or psychological effect. My work with Margo Herr at Harper & Row had been going in that direction and we further explored it. Eventually I did some full color covers and some children's book work for her. I think Margo was most influential in allowing me to grow as an illustrator." (interview by Joachim Boaz)

Doubleday, 1966 / title font: Rubens

In the early sixties Manny co-taught a class at Pratt and mentioned the influence of the students: "They were so free about what they were doing. Some of them were stoned [laughs]. They would say to me, 'Oh, I just dropped some acid, so don't worry if I seem a little strange.'" (From a 2022 interview by Laura McLaws Helms for her Sighs and Whispers podcast)

Doubleday Crime Club Selection, 1967 / title font: Haas Inserat-Grotesk

"I always enjoyed reading the book, good or bad, and getting a feeling for atmosphere more than anything. Then the challenge of bringing design and image together to tell a story without giving too much away. I had an art school training all over the place and came out of Pratt with a portfolio of etchings. I had one instructor, Richard Lindner, who taught me the importance of observation and everything became visual reference. You can probably spot many influences."

Doubleday Science Fiction, 1967 / title font: Information

"Reading was always a great joy for me so being paid to read a book was even better. The important thing about reading the book was that I could not be accused of putting something in the cover art that was not in the story. Also it gave me a framework, and a feeling for atmosphere." (interview by Joachim Boaz)

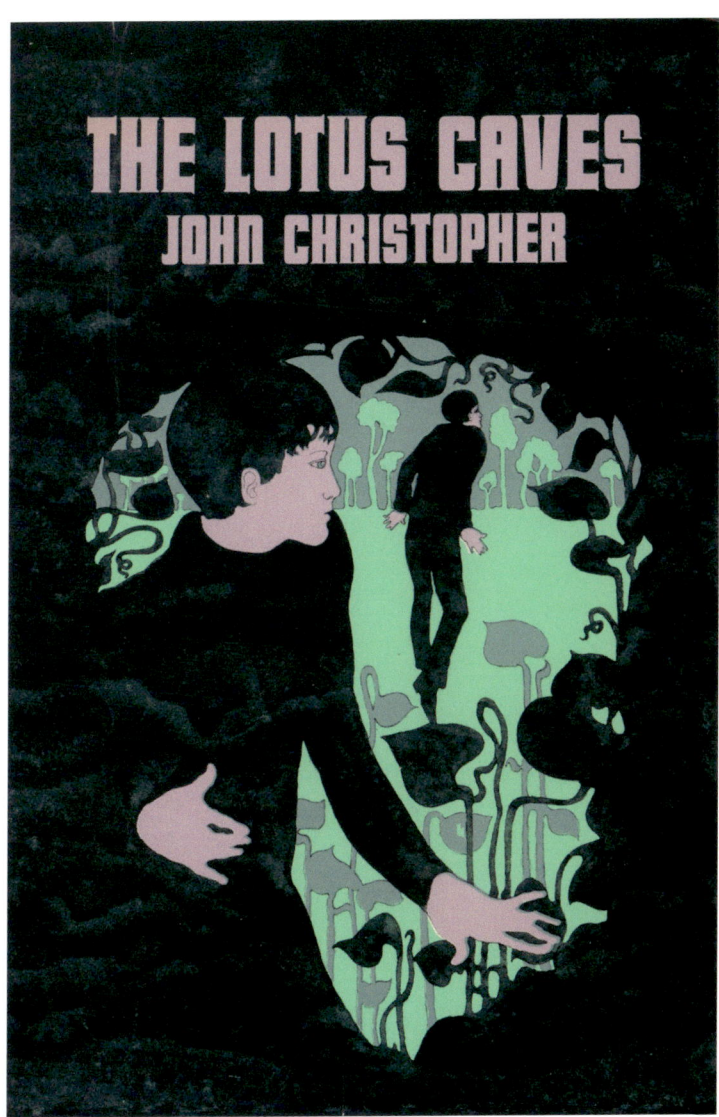

Macmillan, 1969 / title font: Hess Neobold

"Editorial approval for the cover was often more difficult than from the art director. It no longer matters so now I can say, I sometimes chose an obviously clumsy type design for an editor to focus on . . . Satisfied with their input, I could make the change to the originally-planned, more-appropriate typeface. I had saved concept, illustration, and design."

Macmillan, c1969 / title font: Ludlow Radiant Heavy

"At times I do thumbnails but more often full size idea sketches on tracing paper, then layers, tracing refinements, collaging, enlarging, reducing bits and pieces, and manipulating composition. A long sentence and a long process . . . collaging is a pretty loose term here. After I do a preliminary sketch, I cut apart the images and rearrange them, sometimes reducing or enlarging, then tape them down to make a more pleasing composition. The new taped or pasted image is what I call a kind of collage."

Macmillan, c1969 / title font: Venus Extra Bold Extended

"I loved doing illustration, I really loved doing the work. I did not like looking for [work], I did not like the interference very often, which would come from people who were not involved, people above the art director . . . And then there were the editors who would take an art class and they would become sort of 'experts' and start making criticisms or changes." (Sighs and Whispers podcast)

Lothrop, Lee, & Shepard, 1974 / title font: Columna

"As a child I had access to early elementary school readers inherited from an older sister. I still have them and more I have collected through the years, these may really be my roots. The illustrations in the color fairy books and Jessie Willcox Smith illustrations, Japanese prints, art nouveau, art deco, early Disney, early to mid 20th century magazine illustration." (comment on the Animalarium blog)

Lothrop, Lee, & Shepard, 1974 / title font: Columna

In a comment on the Animalarium blog, Manny discussed some of his influences: "I think Heath Robinson (not Charles, always preferred Heath), Rackham, a bit Beardsley, and Howard Pyle. I think Pogany as well, Kay Nielsen, Dorothy Lathrop, maybe Rockwell Kent, and too many more! Jean de Bosschère, the wonderful Boutet de Monvel, and Maud

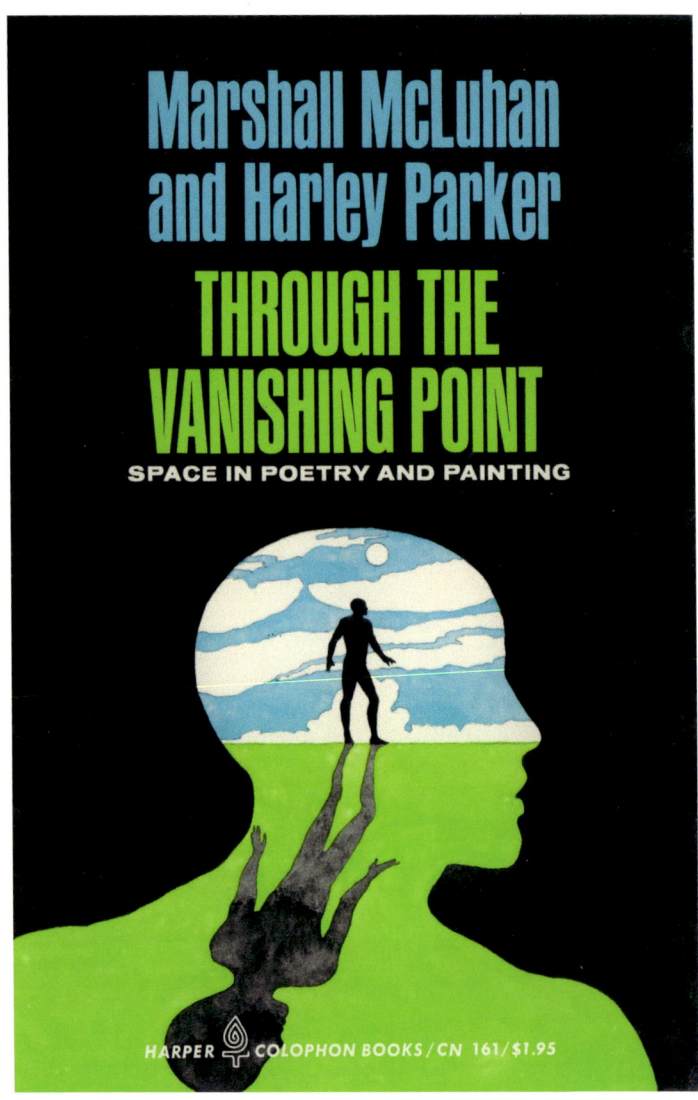

Harper Colophon Books, 1969 / title font: Haas Inserat-Grotesk

"Margo Herr, an art director at Harper and Row, was the first to respond. I did a series of covers for her for a range of paperback books from scholarly to classic. Margo and the editors pretty much gave me the freedom to explore concept and design. After Margo left to go to Doubleday I continued to work with art director Pat Steir, and later Karen Sukoneck with the same degree of freedom." (interview by Joachim Boaz)

Harper Colophon Books, 1968 / title font: Melior Bold Condensed

"I did work with an art director, Margo Herr and later Katherine Hopkins. Margo took a chance on me early on, both she and Katherine gave me the freedom to do as I liked with very little direction. Both believed the choice of artist was the important thing and unless asked gave very little input. The artist was responsible for not only the choice of fonts (called type in those days), but the mechanical, color separations, and paste ups as well."

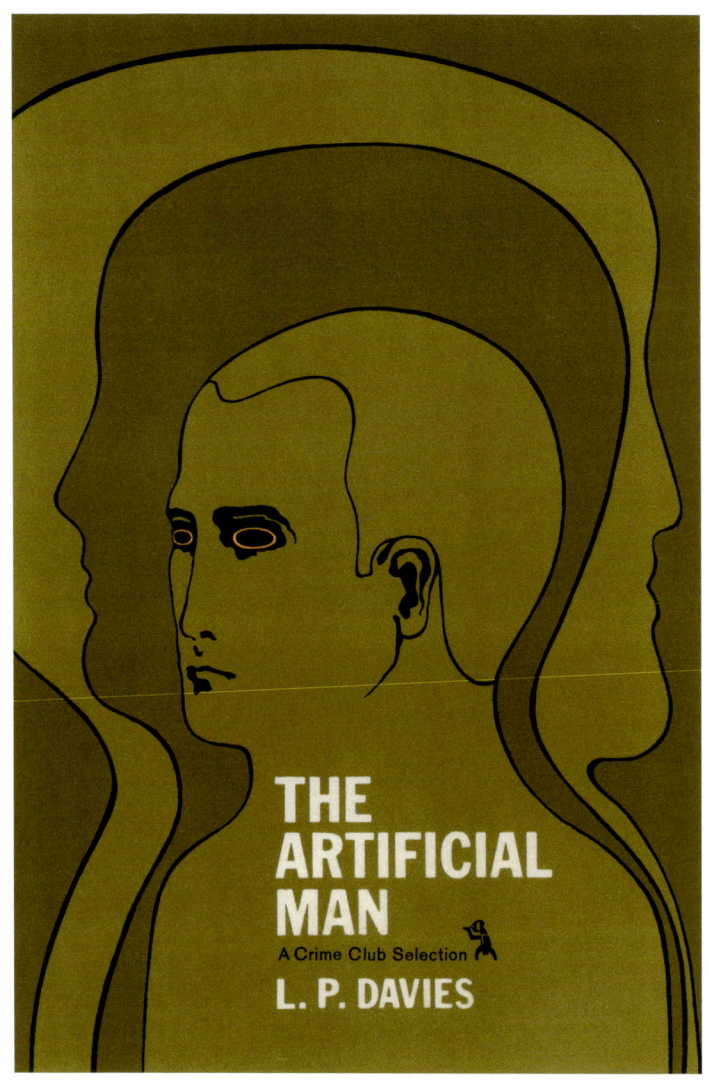

Doubleday Crime Club Selection, 1967 / title font: Franklin Gothic

"For everything I did I was always looking for reference first, it was part of the ceremonial thing. I would look through every book and every magazine I had, just sort of making things cook in my head." (Sighs and Whispers podcast)

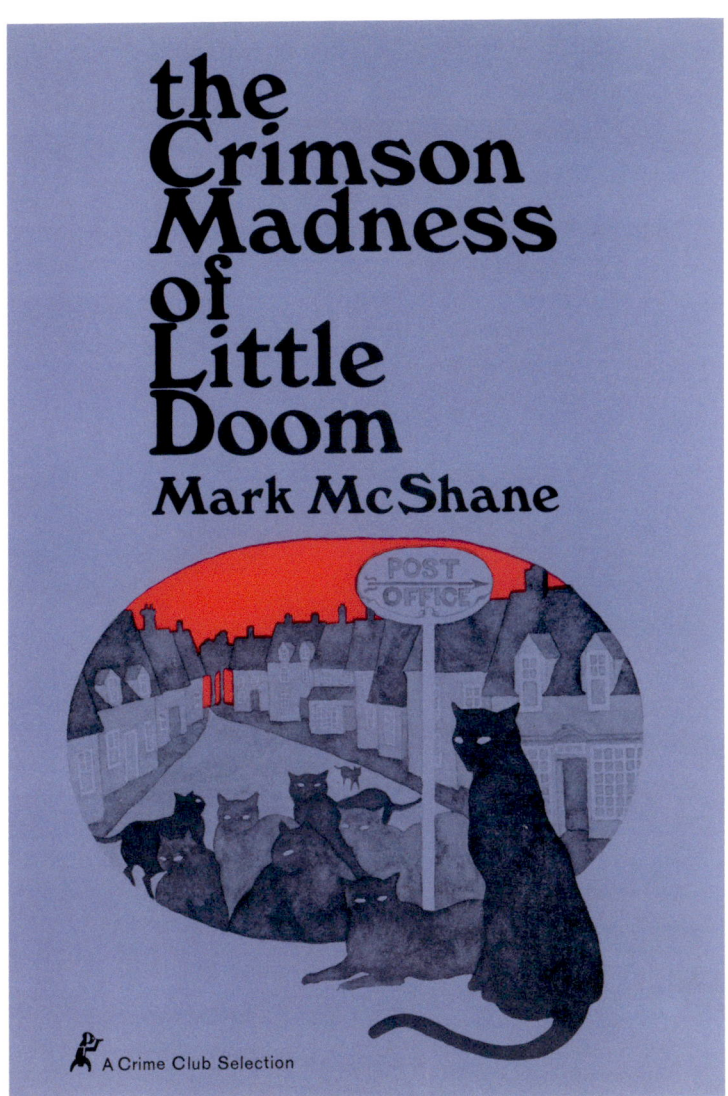

Doubleday Crime Club Selection, 1966 / title font: Windsor

"I enjoy watercolor, I enjoy the challenge; it's not difficult for me . . . that was just always my way of doing it." (Sighs and Whispers podcast)

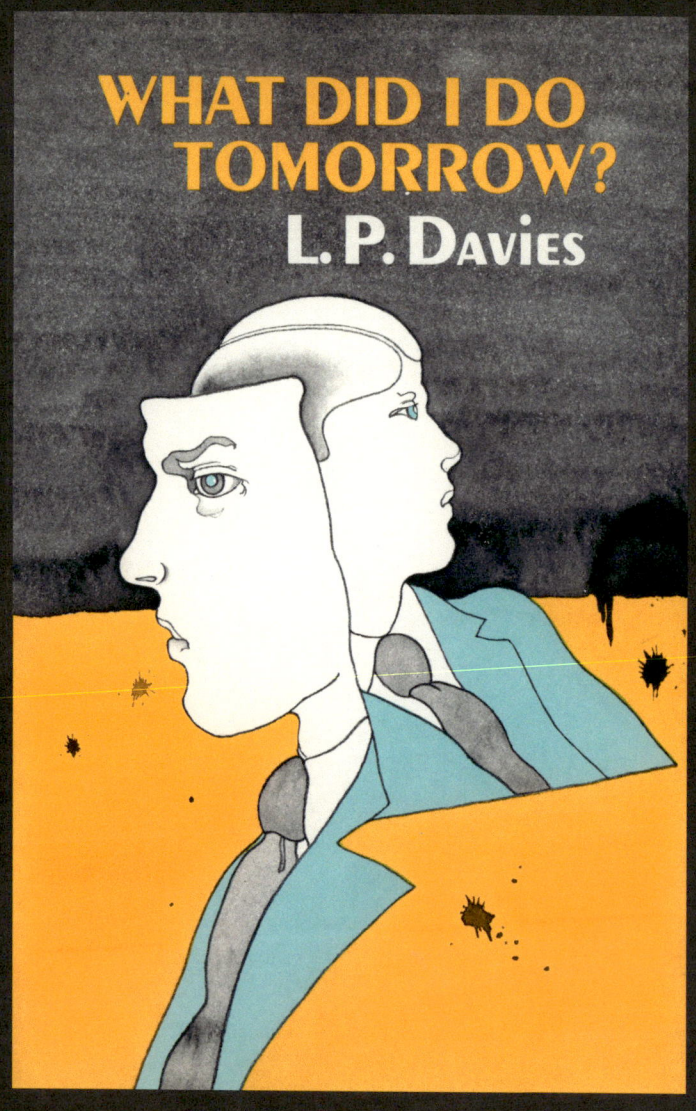

Doubleday Science Fiction, 1973 / title font: Peignot

"I think I enjoyed reading the novels of L. P. Davies most. His novels were in both the SF and Crime Club categories. sometimes a crossover in each. A kind of mystery, fantasy, psychological aspect to each. He asked for me after the first cover and I did his covers for both SF and mystery till I stopped doing covers."

Doubleday Science Fiction, 1968 / title font: Huxley Vertical

Discussing the illustrations in the West German magazine *Twen* (1959-1971, art director Willy Fleckhaus): "I don't know if they influenced me, but I *wanted* them to influence me."

Lothrop, Lee, & Shepard, c1977 / title font: Art Gothic

"I never really hung out with the illustration crowd [laughs]. I was not a member of the Society of Illustrators. I would occasionally be in shows, but only because the work had been submitted by the art director . . . I was not part of that scene."
(Sighs and Whispers podcast)

**Doubleday Crime Club Selection, 1967 / title font:
Century Schoolbook Bold Condensed**

"It does strike me funny now . . . I didn't think of them as trippy at the time. I really have not done a lot of drugs, especially psychedelic drugs I haven't done at all. I have enough trouble keeping up with reality as it is." (Sighs and Whispers podcast)

Doubleday Science Fiction, 1970 / title font: Phenix American

"I would just choose something that I felt was a lead, or something that was a curiosity . . . something that someone would *want* to look into this book for. I also felt that it had to have a graphic kind of feel to it, sort of a poster-y feel to it." (Sighs and Whispers podcast)

Doubleday Science Fiction, 1968 / title font: Orplid

"I don't really know exactly what my influences would have been. I think it may have been from earlier book covers done in the 20s and 30s but also they were three color so there would be a black plate and a two-color plate and I could combine the two colors to make a third color." (Sighs and Whispers podcast)

Doubleday Crime Club Selection, 1968

"I didn't always like choosing the type, but I got to be fairly decent at it, and often would do hand-lettering rather than ordering type." (Sighs and Whispers podcast)

Doubleday Crime Club Selection, 1967

"Finding, or coming up with the idea was part of the solving the problem . . . it was like solving a mystery, finding something that I would be happy with visually, or maybe psychologically and hope that a reader would find the same interest."
(Sighs and Whispers podcast)

Doubleday Crime Club Selection, 1969 / title font: Phoebus

"L. P. Davies was my favorite author to do covers for. His books always had a lovely sort of creepiness, crime, science fiction, fantasy, or a mixture of all. In this book the murder weapon was an award trophy."

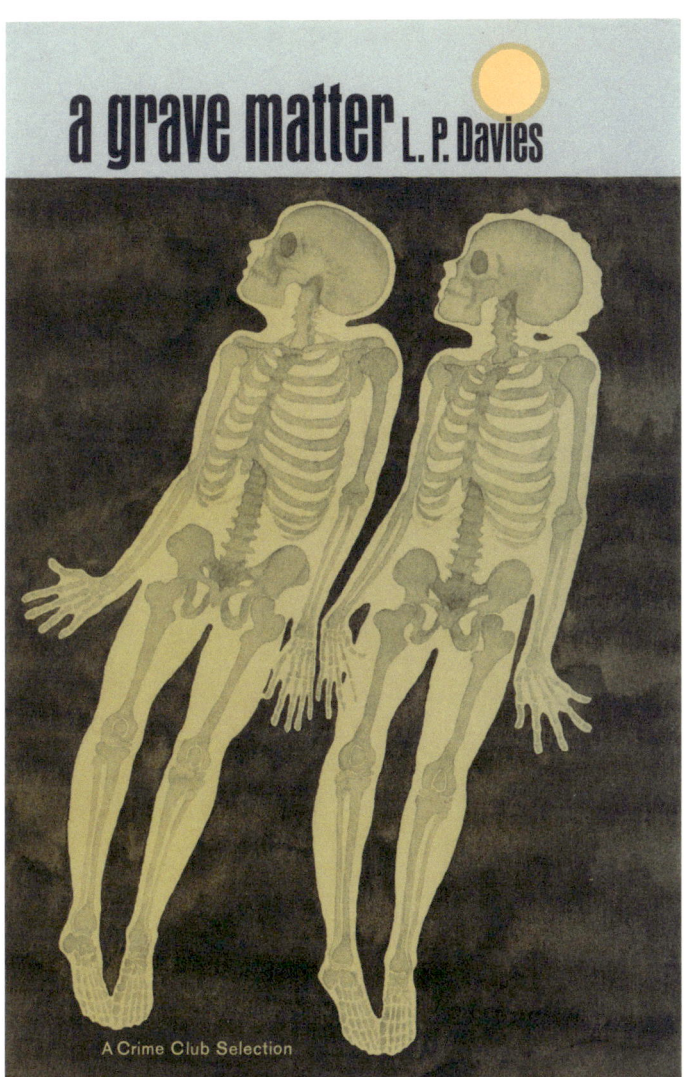

Doubleday Crime Club Selection, 1968 / title font: Haas Inserat-Grotesk

"Most pieces look better today than I thought when I did them. There may be one or two that make me wince. Surprisingly distance improves."

Macmillan, c1969 / title font: Eurostile

"I was never very aggressive about getting work and always was a bit surprised when I did get it. It was still a time when you could actually see an art director and show your work. I stopped doing book jackets when Push Pin started representing me in the 70s, my prices went up."